Guitar Adventures
for Kids

Book & Videos, Level 1   Damon Ferrante

Introduction: *Having Fun with the Guitar!*

How the Book Works

> ❖**Check Out**
> **Video Lesson 1:**
> **Introduction**

The Book

This book and video course for children follows a step-by-step lesson format for learning how to play the guitar. It is designed for beginners and no music experience is necessary to use the book. Each lesson builds on the previous one in a clear and easy-to-understand manner. There are 30 lessons in the book. You learn how to play the guitar through famous songs and pieces.

At the end of the book, you will be able to play the following songs and pieces in easy-guitar arrangements: *Jingle Bells, Skip to My Lou, Ode to Joy, Amazing Grace, When the Saints Go Marching In, Yankee Doodle, Old MacDonald, Take Me Out to the Ballgame, Michael, Row the Boat Ashore, Peace Like a River, Twinkle, Twinkle Little Star*, and many more songs.

The Videos

There are 10 Free, Streaming Video Lessons that coincide with the material presented in *Guitar Adventures for Kids*. The Lesson Videos cover playing songs and pieces, guitar technique, tuning, the parts of the guitar, basic music elements and fundamentals, and how to develop good practice habits. All of these videos are <u>free</u> and available on **<u>Youtube</u>** type **<u>"Kids' Guitar Adventures"</u>**. <u>No</u> Registration or Sign-Up is needed to view the videos and there is no limit to the amount of times that they may be viewed.

Table of Contents

Guitar Adventures for Kids, Level 1:
Fun, Step-by-Step, Beginner
Lesson Guide to Get You Started
(Book & Videos)

by Damon Ferrante

ISBN-13:
978-0615933788 (Steeplechase Arts)

ISBN-10:
0615933785

For additional information about
music books, recordings, and concerts,
please visit the Steeplechase website:
www.steeplechasearts.com

steeplechase
arts & productions

Steeplechase Music Instruction

Also by Damon Ferrante

Guitar Adventures for Kids, Level 2: Fun, Step-by-Step,
Lesson Guide (Book & Videos)

Little Piano Book: Fun, Step-By-Step, Easy-to-Follow, 60-
Lesson Song and Beginner Piano Guide to Get You
Started (Book & Videos)

Guitar Adventures: A Fun, Informative, and Step-By-Step
60-Lesson Guide to Chords, Beginner & Intermediate
Levels, with Companion Lesson and Play-Along Videos

Ultimate Guitar Chords, Scales, & Arpeggios Handbook:
240-Lesson, Step-By-Step, 1-Per-Day, Easy-To-Follow
Guitar Guide (Book & Videos)

Parts of the Guitar

Lesson 1

Here is a Diagram of a Guitar.

Try to find these parts on your guitar. If you have an electric guitar, it might look a little bit different. *Have Fun!*

See Video 1

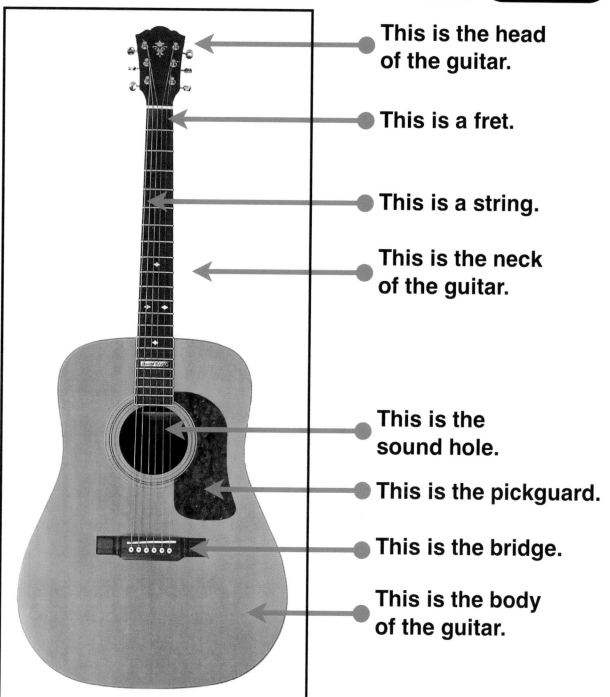

This is the head of the guitar.

This is a fret.

This is a string.

This is the neck of the guitar.

This is the sound hole.

This is the pickguard.

This is the bridge.

This is the body of the guitar.

Names of the Strings

In this lesson, we are going to learn about the letter names for the guitar strings.

See Video 2

Low High
E A D G B E

The Guitar Strings

- 6th String, **Low E = Every**
- 5th String, A = **Alligator**
- 4th String, D = **Drinks**
- 3rd String, G = **Grape Juice**
- 2nd String, B = **Before**
- 1st String, High E = **Eating**

- The guitar has six strings.
- The strings have numbers that go from the thinnest string to the thickest string.
- The thinnest string is string #1. It is located closest to the floor and it has the highest sound.
- The thickest string is string #6. It is located closest to the ceiling and has the lowest (or deepest) sound.
- The thinnest string (the first string) is called the "High E String".
- The thickest string (the sixth string) is called the "Low E String".

- Going from thickest string to thinnest string, here are the letter names for the strings:
  Low E, A, D, G, B, High E.
- To help you remember the letter names and order for the strings, here is a funny sentence: Every Alligator Drinks Grape Juice Before Eating.
- The first letter of each word (**except for "juice"**) stands for a string of the guitar, going from thickest string to thinnest string. **See the chart on the left.**

Holding the Guitar

Lesson 3

First, let's find a comfortable chair or couch and sit down with the guitar.

To hold the guitar, put the guitar on your right leg, in your lap. Then, place your right hand over the front of the guitar body, so that your hand is in front of the sound hole. Bring your left hand under the guitar neck and gently place your fingers over the strings.

Now, you're ready to make some great music and have fun!

Try Playing the open Strings for this song.
The E String is Blue. The B String is Orange.

At the Starting Line

E E B B | E E E E | E E B B | E E E E ‖

Holding the Guitar Pick

Lesson 4

See Video 3

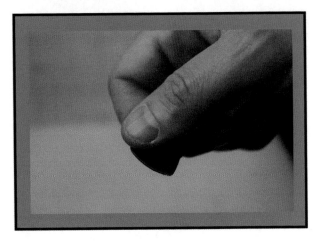

Let's now look at how to hold the guitar pick.

- Gently place the guitar pick on the finger nail of your Right-Hand Index Finger.
- It should be resting gently on top of your finger nail.
- Then, slide it to the left side of your Index Finger.
- Finally, gently place your Right-Hand Thumb over over the guitar pick. It should be held between your Right-Hand Thumb and Index Finger.

Try Playing the open Strings for this song.
The E String is Blue.
The B String is Orange.

Race Cars

EEBB | EEEE | BBEE | BEEE ||

 Joke Time! "Knock, Knock." "Who's There?" "Lettuce"."
"Lettuce, who?" "Let us in; it's lunchtime." Ha! Ha!

Left-Hand Position

Lesson 5

See Video 4

Now, let's learn about how to use the left hand when we play the guitar. It's important to always play on the tips of our left-hand fingers, when we press down a string to make a note on the guitar. If we don't use the tips of our left-hand fingers, we may miss the note, play an "extra / wrong" note, or make the string buzz. *Check Out Video 4 to see this technique.*

Try Playing the open Strings for this song.
The E String is Blue. The B String is Orange.
The 3rd String (the G String) is Purple.

Mountain Sunrise

E E B B | G G G G | B B B B | E E E E ||

Notes on the 1st String

Lesson 6

Let's learn 3 Notes on the 1st String.
E is the Open String: No Left Hand Needed.
F is on the 1st Fret. Use your Index Finger.
G is on the 3rd Fret. Use your Ring Finger.

See Video 5

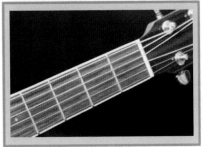

E
The Open 1st String

F
1st Fret of the
1st String

G
3rd Fret of the
1st String

Try this song that uses 3 notes on the 1st String.
E is Blue. F is Green. G is Red. **Have Fun!**

Fun Balloons

E E G G | E E E E | E E F F | E E E E ||

Joke Time! "What did the Teddy Bear say after dinner?"
"No dessert for me; I'm stuffed." Ha! Ha! Ha!

Songs on the 1st String

Try these songs that use 3 notes on the 1st String.
E is Blue. F is Green. G is Red. **Have Fun!**

Jogging Puppy

Lesson 7

G G G E | F F F E | G E F E ||

Check Out Video Lesson 6 for help tuning the guitar

See Video 6

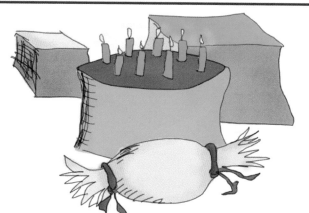

Birthday Fun

E G E G | F G F G | G F E E | F E E E ||

Joke Time! "What space villain works at a restaurant?"
"Darth Waiter! " Ha! Ha! Ha!

Counting & Measures

Lesson 8

- Music is composed of groups of beats called measures.
- Measures are set off by vertical lines, called bar lines.
- Measures most commonly contain 2, 3, or 4 beats.
- Below, are examples of sets of four measures in 4/4 time.
- In 4/4 time, you will count 4 beats for each measure.
  In other words, you will count: 1234, 1234, 1234, 1234.
- Try counting aloud and clapping the beats for the exercise below.

Example 1:

| 1 2 3 4 | 1 2 3 4 | 1 2 3 4 | 1 2 3 4 ‖

Example 2:
Try Clapping on the X: On the First Beat.

| 1 2 3 4 | 1 2 3 4 | 1 2 3 4 | 1 2 3 4 ‖
| X | X | X | X

Example 3:
Try Clapping on the X: On the First and Third Beats.

| 1 2 3 4 | 1 2 3 4 | 1 2 3 4 | 1 2 3 4 ‖
| X   X | X   X | X   X | X   X

Example 4:
Try Clapping on the X: On the Second Beat.

| 1 2 3 4 | 1 2 3 4 | 1 2 3 4 | 1 2 3 4 ‖
| X | X | X | X

Notes on the 2nd String

Lesson 9

Let's learn 3 Notes on the 2nd String.
B is the Open String: No Left Hand Needed.
C is on the 1st Fret. Use your Index Finger.
D is on the 3rd Fret. Use your Ring Finger.

See Video 7

B
The Open 2nd String

C
1st Fret of the
2nd String

D
3rd Fret of the
2nd String

*Try this song that uses **3 Notes** on the **2nd String**.*
*B is Orange. C is Green. D is Purple. **Have Fun!***

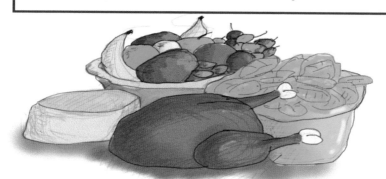

Thanksgiving Dinner

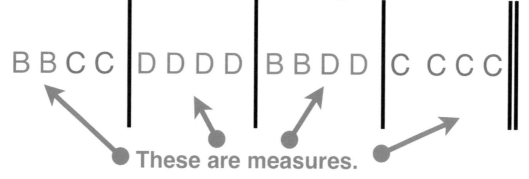

B B C C | D D D D | B B D D | C C C C ||

These are measures.

Songs on 2nd String

Lesson 10

Try these songs that use **3 Notes** on the **2nd String**. *B is Orange. C is Green. D is Purple.* **Have Fun!**

Bouncing Ball

C C B B | D D D D | C C B B | C C C C ‖

Rocket Ship

C C C C | D D D D | B B B B | C C C C ‖

Lesson 11 · Time Signatures

- Measures are composed of groups of beats called Time Signatures or Meter (both terms mean the same thing and are interchangeable).
- The most common Time Signatures (or "meters") are groups of 2, 3, or 4 beats per measure: 2/4, 3/4, and 4/4 Time Signatures.
- 2/4 Time Signature groups the notes into measures of 2 beats. Count: "One, Two" for each measure.
- 3/4 Time Signature groups the notes into measures of 3 beats. Count: "One, Two, Three" for each measure.
- 4/4 Time Signature groups the notes into measures of 4 beats. Count: "One, Two, Three, Four" for each measure.
- Below, are examples of sets of four measures in 2/4, 3/4, and 4/4.
- Count aloud and clap on the first beat for the exercises below.

Example 1: 2/4 Time Signature
Try Clapping on the **X**: On the First Beat.

$\frac{2}{4}$	1 2	1 2	1 2	1 2
	X	X	X	X

Example 2: 3/4 Time Signature
Try Clapping on the X: On the First Beat.

$\frac{3}{4}$	1 2 3	1 2 3	1 2 3	1 2 3
	X	X	X	X

Example 3: 4/4 Time Signature
Try Clapping on the X: On the First Beat.

$\frac{4}{4}$	1 2 3 4	1 2 3 4	1 2 3 4	1 2 3 4
	X	X	X	X

Songs on 1st & 2nd Strings

Lesson 12

*Try these songs that use **3 Notes** on the **1st and 2nd Strings**. **E** is **Blue**. **F** is **Brown**. **G** is **Red**. **B** is **Orange**. **C** is **Green**. **D** is **Purple**.*

Have Fun!

Mary's Little Lamb

$\frac{4}{4}$ | E D C D | E E E | D D D | E G G
Ma-ry had a | lit- tle lamb | lit- tle lamb | lit- tle lamb

Here is the Time Signature

E D C D | E E E E D | D E D | C
Ma-ry had a | lit- tle lamb its | fleece was white as | snow

Skip to My Lou

$\frac{4}{4}$ E E C C | E E G | D D B B | D D F

E E C C | E E G | D F E D | C C

Songs on 1st & 2nd Strings

Lesson 13

Try these songs that use **3 Notes** on the **1st and 2nd Strings**. E is **Blue**. F is **Brown**. G is **Red**. B is *Orange*. C is *Green*. D is *Purple*.

Have Fun!

Ode to Joy

$\frac{4}{4}$ E E F G | G F E D | C C D E | E D D |

E E F G | G F E D | C C D E | D C C |

Jingle Bells

$\frac{4}{4}$ E E E | E E E | E G C D | E |

Jin-gle Bells, | Jin-gle Bels | Jin-gle all the | way.

F F F F | F E E E | E D D E | D G |

Oh, what fun it | is to ride on a | one horse open | sleigh. Hey!

Whole Notes, Half Notes, and Quarter Notes

Lesson 14

- Let's take a look at some basic rhythms.
- Quarter Notes are notes that get 1 Beat (or Count).
- Half Notes are notes that get 2 Beats (or Counts).
- Whole Notes are notes that get 4 Beats (or Counts).
- In the next 3 examples, try counting on each beat of the 4/4 measures aloud, for example: 1,2,3,4.
- Clap on the quarter, half, and whole notes.

♩ = 1 Beat   ♩ = 2 Beats   o = 4 Beats

Example 1:
Try Clapping on each "**X**", while counting the beats.

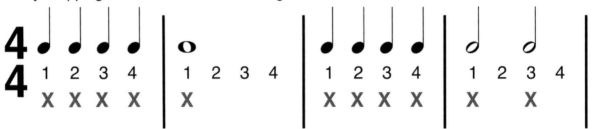

Example 2:
Try Clapping on each "**X**", while counting the beats.

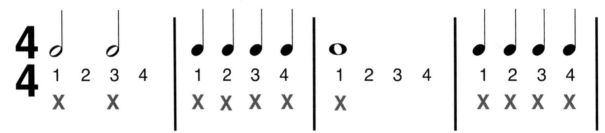

Example 3:
Try Clapping on each "**X**", while counting the beats.

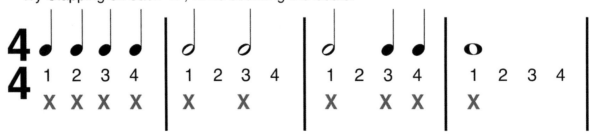

Whole Notes & Half Notes

Lesson 15

*Try these songs that use **3 Notes** on the **1st String**.*
E is Blue. F is Brown. G is Red.

Have Fun!

O Whole Note = 4 Beats

For Whole Notes Count: 1,2, 3, 4
For Half Notes Count: 1, 2

Half Note = 2 Beats

The Happy Cat

4
4

O   ♩   ♩   O

F   G   F   G

Beats: 1 2 3 4   1 2 3 4   1 2 3 4

Raindrops

4
4   ♩ ♩   ♩ ♩   ♩ ♩   ♩ ♩   ♩ ♩

G E   G G   G E   G E   G G

Beats: 1 2 3 4   1 2 3 4   1 2 3 4   1 2 3 4   1 2 3 4

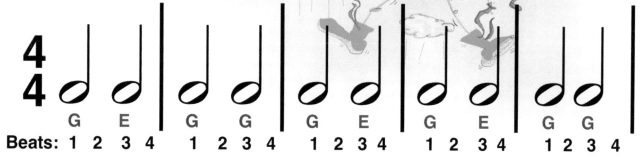

More Songs with Whole & Half Notes

Lesson 16

Try these songs that use **3 Notes** on the **1st and 2nd Strings**.
E is Blue. F is Brown. G is Red.
B is Orange. C is Green. D is Purple.

Have Fun!

Turtles Walking

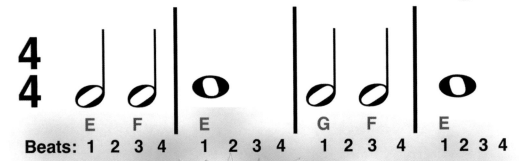

	E	F	E		G	F	E

Beats: 1 2 3 4   1 2 3 4   1 2 3 4   1 2 3 4

Sunny Day

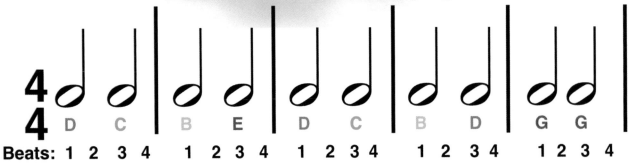

D C   B E   D C   B D   G G

Beats: 1 2 3 4   1 2 3 4   1 2 3 4   1 2 3 4   1 2 3 4

Songs with Quarter Notes & Half Notes

Lesson 17

Try these songs that use **3 Notes** on the **1st and 2nd Strings**.
E is Blue. F is Brown. G is Red.
B is Orange. C is Green. D is Purple.

Have Fun!

Moonlight

Sleepy Chair

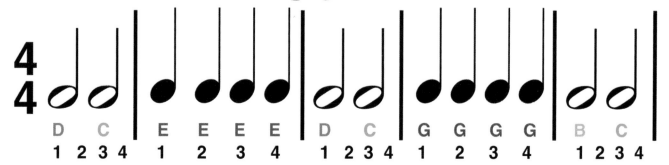

Songs with Quarter Notes, Half Notes & Whole Notes

Lesson 18

Try these songs that use **3 Notes** on the **1st and 2nd Strings**. *E is Blue. F is Brown. G is Red. B is Orange. C is Green. D is Purple.*

Have Fun!

Jazz Band

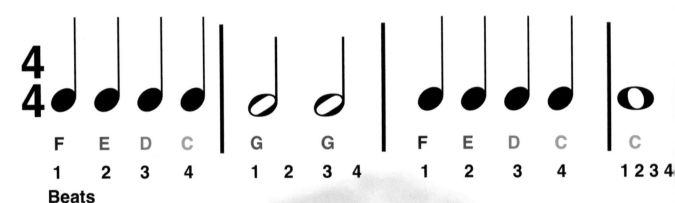

F E D C G G F E D C C

1 2 3 4 1 2 3 4 1 2 3 4 1 2 3 4

Beats

Bells Ringing

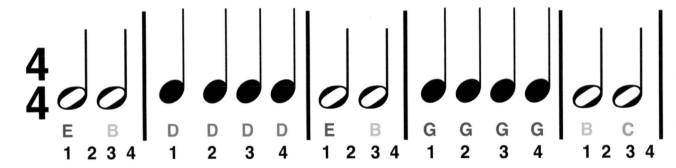

E B D D D D E B G G G G B C

1 2 3 4 1 2 3 4 1 2 3 4 1 2 3 4 1 2 3 4

Notes on the 3rd String

Lesson 19

Let's learn 2 Notes on the 3rd String.
G is the Open String: No Left Hand Needed.
A is on the 2nd Fret. Use your Middle Finger.

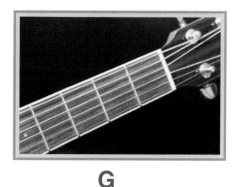

G

The Open 3rd String

A

2nd Fret of the
3rd String

Happy Letters

See Video 8

$\frac{4}{4}$ G G G G | A A A A | G G G G | G G A A ‖

Songs on the 3rd String

Lesson 20

Let's learn two songs that use notes from the 3rd String: G and A.

G is **Blue**
A is **Red**

Ice Cream Time

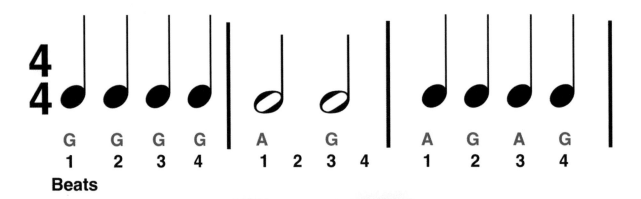

Clouds

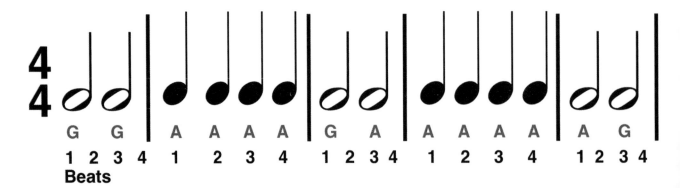

Songs on 3 Strings

Lesson 21

Let's try two new songs that use 2 and 3 strings. In "Yankee Doodle", the **Blue G** and the **Red A** are on the 3rd String (the G String). *Have Fun!*

Old MacDonald

C	C	C	G	A	A	G	E	E	D	D	C
Old	Mac-	Don-	ald	had	a	farm.	E-	I-	E -	I-	O !

C	C	C	G	A	A	G	E	E	D	D	C
On	his	farm	he	had	a	cow.	E-	I-	E -	I-	O !

Yankee Doodle

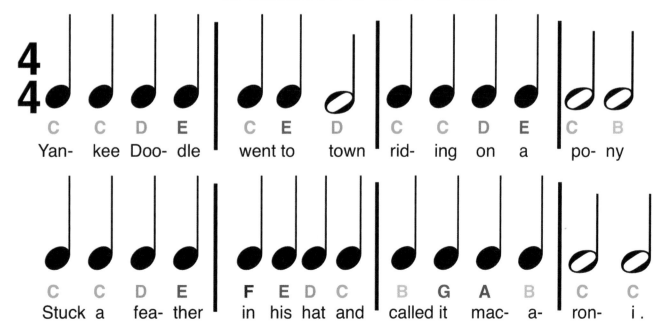

C	C	D	E	C	E	D	C	C	D	E	C	B
Yan-	kee	Doo-	dle	went	to	town	rid-	ing	on	a	po-	ny

C	C	D	E	F	E	D	C	B	G	A	B	C	C
Stuck	a	fea-	ther	in	his	hat	and	called	it	mac-	a-	ron-	i .

A Song on 3 Strings

Lesson 22

Try this song that is on strings 1, 2, and 3: the High E String, the B String, and the G String.
The **Blue** "**G**" and the **Black** "**A**" are on the 3rd String.

Remember to Count the Beats.

Have Fun!

Michael, Row the Boat Ashore

Beats

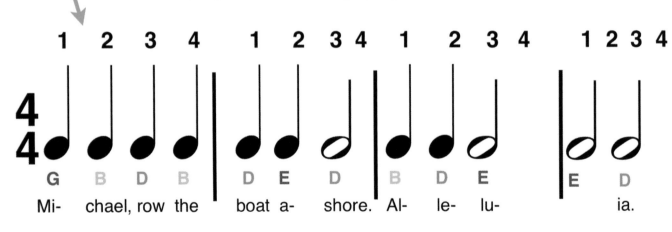

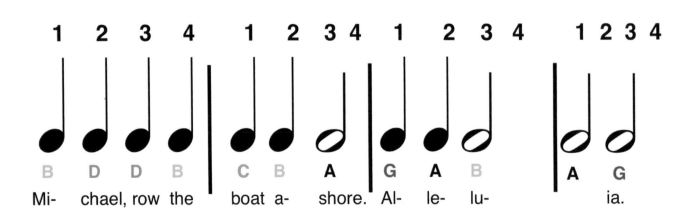

Notes on the 4th String

Lesson 23

Let's learn 3 Notes on the 4th String.
D is the Open String: No Left Hand Needed.
E is on the 2nd Fret. Use your Index Finger.
F is on the 3rd Fret. Use your Middle Finger.

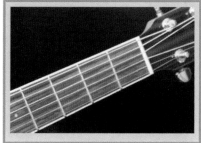

D
The Open 4th String

E
2nd Fret of the
4th String

F
3rd Fret of the
4th String

Tennis Fun

See Video 9

$\frac{4}{4}$

F	D	E	D	D	D	F	D	E	F	D	D	E	D
1	2 3	4	1	2	3	4	1	2 3	4	1	2	3	4	1	2 3	4

A Song on the D String

Lesson 24

Try this song that uses
3 Notes on the **4th String**.
D is **Blue**.
E is **Purple**.
F is **Red**.
Have Fun!

Beats

Surfing the Waves

Songs on 3 & 4 Strings

Lesson 25

Try these songs that use 3 & 4 Strings.
The **Blue "G"** and **Red "A"** are on the 3rd String.

Twinkle, Twinkle, Little Star

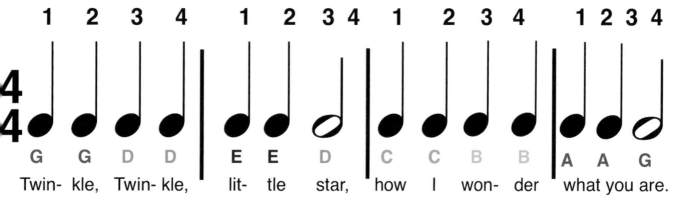

1	2	3	4	1	2	3	4	1	2	3	4	1	2	3	4
G	G	D	D	E	E	D		C	C	B	B	A	A	G	
Twin-	kle,	Twin-	kle,	lit-	tle	star,		how	I	won-	der		what you are.		

We have a new kind of note:
The Dotted Half Note.
It is equal to 3 Beats (or Counts)
Can you point to some Dotted Half
Notes in *At the Ballpark?*

𝅗𝅥. = 3 Beats

At the Ballpark

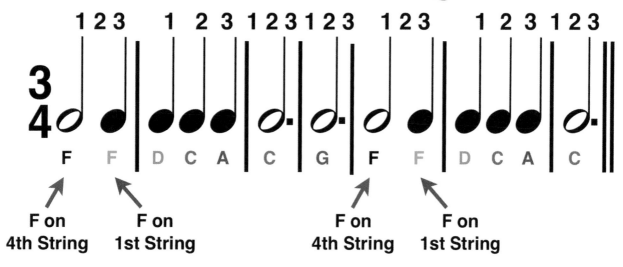

1 2 3	1 2 3	1 2 3	1 2 3	1 2 3	1 2 3	1 2 3	1 2 3
F	F D C A	C	G	F	F D C A	C	

F on
4th String

F on
1st String

F on
4th String

F on
1st String

Let's Learn Some Guitar Chords

Strumming Chords

In this lesson, we are going to begin learning about playing chords.
Chords are groups of 3 or more notes that are played at the same time.
In *Guitar Adventures for Kids, Level 1*, we are going to learn 4 songs that
use chords. In *Guitar Adventures for Kids, Level 2*, we are going to learn
many more songs that use chords and strumming techniques.
Take some time to look over the chord symbols on this page.

Lesson 26

Left-Hand Symbols:

1 • 1st Finger (Index Finger)

2 • 2nd Finger (Middle Finger)

3 • 3rd Finger (Ring Finger)

4 • 4th Finger (Pinky Finger)

O • **Open String**
(Let the String Vibrate.)

X • **Mute String**
(Block the String with a Finger.)

1 • **Place Finger
over 2 or more
strings.**

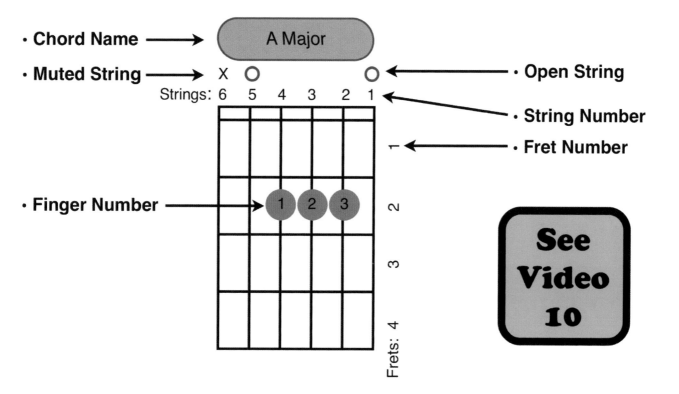

• **Chord Name** ⟶   A Major

• **Muted String** ⟶ X O   O ⟵ • **Open String**

Strings: 6 5 4 3 2 1 ⟵ • **String Number**

1 ⟵ • **Fret Number**

• **Finger Number** ⟶ ① ② ③

Frets: 4

See Video 10

The C Major Chord & G Major Chord

In this lesson, we are going to learn two new chords: C Major and G Major (see the diagrams). Remember to place the tips of your left-hand fingers on the strings when you play chords. Try playing 4 down-strums for each measure.

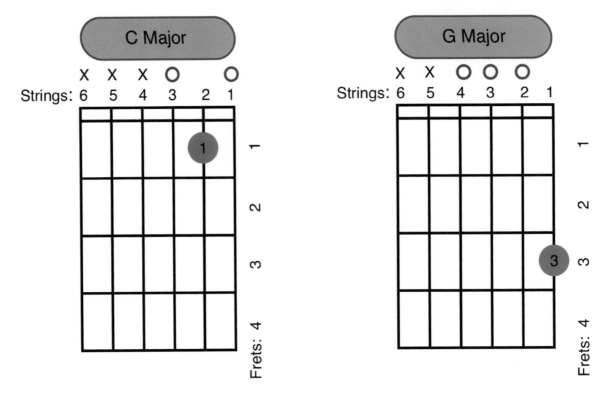

Rock & Roll Time!

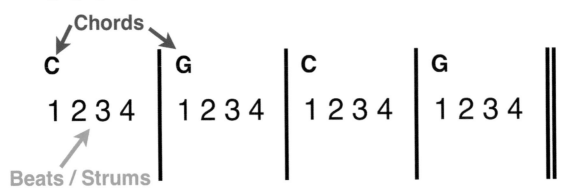

The F Major Chord

Lesson 28

Let's look at a new chord: F Major. It uses only 2 strings: the 1st & 2nd.

In *Peace Like a River,* we have three chords: C, F, and G.

Begin strumming on the second full measure (during the word "peace").

Have Fun!

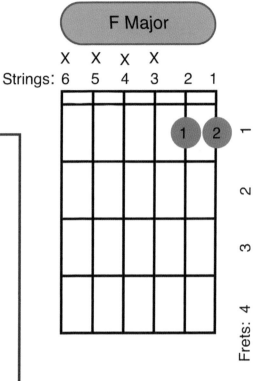

F Major

Strings: X X X X
6 5 4 3 2 1

1 2

Frets: 4 3 2 1

Peace Like a River

Chord:	(No Chord)	C	C	F
	I've got	peace like a	river. I've got	Peace like a
Strum:	1 2 3 4	1 2 3 4	1 2 3 4	1 2 3 4
Chord: C		C	C	G
	river. I've got	peace like a	river in my	soul.
Strum:	1 2 3 4	1 2 3 4	1 2 3 4	1 2 3 4
Chord: G		C	C	F
	I've got	Peace like a	river. I've got	peace like a
Strum:	1 2 3 4	1 2 3 4	1 2 3 4	1 2 3 4
Chord: C		C	G	C
	river. I've got	peace like a	river in my	soul.
Strum:	1 2 3 4	1 2 3 4	1 2 3 4	1 2 3 4

Amazing Grace

Amazing Grace, has three beats in each measure.
Strum the chords three times per measure.
If you have a question about how to play a chord,
look back at the charts on the previous few pages.

Lesson 29

Amazing Grace

Measure Line

Chord:	C	C	F	C
	A-mazing	Grace how	sweet the	sound that
Strum:	1　2　3	1　2　3	1　2　3	1　2　3
Chord:	C	C	G	G
	saved a	wretch like	me.	I
Strum:	1　2　3	1　2　3	1　2　3	1　2　3
Chord:	C	C	F	C
	once was	lost but	now am	found. Was
Strum:	1　2　3	1　2　3	1　2　3	1　2　3
Chord:	C	G	C	C
	blind but	now I	see.	
Strum:	1　2　3	1　2　3	1　2　3	1　2　3

The C7 Chord

Lesson 30

Great Job on Finishing the Book!

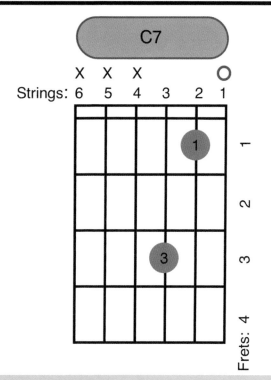

Let's look at the C7 chord.

It is played on three strings.

Make sure that you avoid playing the 4th, 5th, & 6th strings, when you are playing the C7 chord.

Can you find the C7 chord in *When the Saints*?

When the Saints

Chord:	(No Chord)	C	C	C
	Oh When the	Saints	go marchin'	in
Strum:	1　2　3　4	1　2　3　4	1　2　3　4	1　2　3　4

Chord: C		C	C7	G
	Oh When the	Saints go	marchin'	in
Strum: 1	2　3　4	1　2　3　4	1　2　3　4	1　2　3　4

Chord: G		C	C7	F
	Oh　Lord, I	want　　to	be　　in　that	number
Strum: 1	2　3　4	1　2　3　4	1　2　3　4	1　2　3　4

Chord: F		C	G	C
	Oh When the	Saints go	marchin'	in
Strum: 1	2　3　4	1　2　3　4	1　2　3　4	1　2　3　4

Lesson Checklist: Page 1

Use this Checklist to Keep Track of Your Progress:

Lesson #	Completed / Check	Date
1		
2		
3		
4		
5		
6		
7		
8		
9		
10		
11		
12		
13		
14		
15		
16		
17		
18		
19		
20		

Lesson Checklist: Page 2

Use this Checklist to Keep Track of Your Progress:

Lesson #	Completed / Check	Date
21		
22		
23		
24		
25		
26		
27		
28		
29		
30		

CERTIFICATE
of ACCOMPLISHMENT

This certifies that

_____

(sign your name)

*Has successfully completed the training
program requirement for*

GUITAR ADVENTURES FOR KIDS, LEVEL ONE

and is ready to begin

GUITAR ADVENTURES FOR KIDS, LEVEL TWO

_____   _____
DATE   TEACHER

GREAT JOB!

Available in 2014!

Guitar Adventures for Kids

Book & Videos, Level 2   Damon Ferrante

Have Fun Learning Piano!

Little Piano Book

Fun, Step-By-Step, Easy-To-Follow, 60-Lesson
Song and Beginner Piano Guide to Get You Started

Book & Videos

Damon Ferrante

Made in the USA
Lexington, KY
11 February 2014